REBUILDING
T
H
E
W
A
L
L
S

TO YOUR CITY
(YOUR PERSON)

A Reckoning of The Past,

And The

Dawning Of A New Beginning

C. S. Bayliss

TABLE OF CONTENTS

PART III

<u>Dedication</u>

This book is dedicated to my parents, Michael, and
Mom Norman for their inspiration and work ethic;
and to my children - the next generation.

Forward

This book progressed at a snail's pace. It was periodically lying in limbo, making subsequently large, then very small steps toward completion. The desire was clear. The method was in place. The specific mission was lacking. Clarity then knocked on the door.

I attended the home-going service of a woman in her late 40's. This woman was well known for her 'happy-go-lucky' demeanor and her thirst for fun. She enjoyed interacting with various people and having a 'good time'. Through a series of ill-informed choices, emotional abandonment, loss of love, and stagnation perpetuated by a sense of helplessness; this woman's body lay lifeless signaling the untimely end of her existence. You see her keen desire for fun, affection, and affirmation led her into the arms of impulsive decisions, the tentacles of other's baggage, and an overwhelming sense of feeling 'stuck'.

With a beautiful baby face and a soft smile, she was welcomed by many. This process developed in her early teens and took a deeper root in her twenties. This woman's existence was defined by the attention and approval of others. The walls to her city, (the perimeter around her 'being'), were systematically broken down with every disapproval, disappointment, disillusionment, abandonment, and gripping webs of entanglements. She could not turn back or retrace her steps because she had unwittingly torn down the bridges. Now she was stuck in the quagmire, lacking the courage to look in the mirror and draw on the resident beauty and strength of purpose within. She was totally oblivious to the fact that her current situation did not define her life's existence. She yet had purpose & worth, but the connection was not made between the proper support and rebuilding the 'walls to her city'. Instead, yet another life was lost.

How often does this scenario replay in the lives of others, both males and females of different ages? The situations may vary, but the sense of helplessness and /or disillusionment remains. Yes, the mission is now clear. Spread the word, LET'S WIN!!!

Introduction

Twenty-seven-year-old Alexandria, secure in her beauty, knowledge, finances, and a trusting relationship, becomes entangled in the gripping web of depression following heart-searing injustices. Why? What prevents her from taking hold of the strength and potential for success that lies within her and moving forward?

Ronald divorces Stacy after several years of marriage leaving their fifteen-year-old daughter Sabrina confused and bewildered. Ronald was established in his faith, homeownership, and career. He now begins a second family. Why? What were the signs/clues of the impending separation? What needs to be changed to discourage a repetitive cycle of broken relationships?

Thirty-two-year-old Marcia who is full of life, beauty, vitality, knowledge, and hope experiences a large dose of reality's incongruities resulting in her release of certain dreams and boundaries. As she gazes at her reflection in the mirror: noting hair thinning and pronounced weight gain; the decision must be made to either continue in martyrdom and challenged health, or allow her Maker to assist her in restoring the order, respect, and self-discipline to her life.

This list goes on and on. Countless individuals have begun their walk in life with seemingly everything going for them, only to have life's challenges or harshness douse their hopes and influence them to follow a lesser route. Must one continue on a route of defeat or disillusionment? No! One can <u>*choose*</u> to get on track and pursue their Creator's plan and purpose for their life. Determine if it is too late. The choice is ours.

This is not a "How To" book. There are plenty already in print. This is also not a doctrinal dissertation. This book is an *encouraging pat on the shoulder, or a nudge* which suggests that forward progress may yet be within reach, despite our losses, mistakes, feeling of being 'stuck', 'false starts', etc. This prose is informative and supportive. If this book is *thought provoking*, that is good. If this book is *action provoking*, that's even better. Tools for rebuilding are provided. The will to rebuild the walls to our city lies within us.

PART I
City Walls

Take this and that! Health concerns, financial challenges, relationship stressors, child struggles, and other situations occur in multiples seemingly about the same time. Choices! Choices! Choices! What should I do? How, when, or where should this be done? What about the way I feel? What about what I want?

We sometimes make choices that weaken our personal and/or familial structures. The outer boundaries we know as the area surrounding our personal and/or familial space can be referred to as the *'walls to our cities'*. Our acts of commission or omission may result in outside parties having more authority or influence over our lives than we would like (i.e., hospitalizations, forced moves, family separations, etc.); thereby, impacting these boundaries or walls.

I have seen several individuals in my career and personal life who have found themselves in a city without walls. They no longer had the delight of companionship, the liberty of unsupervised movement, the fulfillment of nurturing their own children, or the freedom of pursuing their own desired goals. Instead, the actions or omissions of these individuals have resulted in broken relationships, incarceration, children being reared outside of the homes of their parents, homelessness, and the like. Someone else is now determining what some of his/her future actions must be.

It is clear that when one's city walls have been broken down or destroyed, others then have the opportunity to come into that city and exercise control or influence over that individual's, or that family's affairs. Often, these persons have not heeded physical, spiritual, social, or environmental boundaries. I am sure that some individuals now realize that better judgment, impulse control, disciplined lifestyles, respect for authority, etc. would have been a more desirable course of action. One's focal point at this time is of key importance. It would naturally seem like a comfortable time to get the "Why me?" "Why now?" questions answered.

However, the reality is that dwelling on these questions, at this point, simply delays the growth process of one's time of development, testing, and challenges. A more important focal point would be one's attitude and perception in one's current situation. Consider the following:

I'm Coming Out of This

I'm coming out of this apathy, oppression, depression, lack, poverty, "just missed it," "couldn't help it," "backward stepping," "can't see it," "can't hear it," "can't do it," etc. mentality. With the help and grace of my Maker, I'm coming out of this mindset, these circumstances or conditions.

Do these thoughts sound familiar? Have you come to know similar thoughts? Do you know someone with similar circumstances? If so, please keep reading. The message of this book is that (in the absence of extenuating circumstances) you can be effective in *rebuilding the walls to your city*. If life's circumstances and conditions have left you vulnerable and/or depleted of resources, restoration may yet be possible. *Let's Win!*

Do Not Count Yourself Out

It is extremely easy at times to focus on our inadequacies and shortcomings rather than on our strengths. This particular mindset lends support to us remaining in our comfort zones rather than pressing forward to our goals. This is the *"I can't"* mentality. *I can't interact with Corporate America because... I can't interact with my loved ones because... I can't become an effective parent, public speaker, etc. because... I can't develop or maintain quality relationships because... I can't respect time because... I can't pursue my goals because...* You know the song.

People of this mindset spend more time comparing themselves with others rather than taking the time to affirm and nurture the jewel within them. Do not think of yourself as having less worth than anyone else does. Yes, everyone's lives are different. You may not be in your ideal position or status at this moment, but do not count yourself out. There could possibly be some definite good in your situation and endeavors (even if it's only a dissatisfaction that is pushing you to change for the better).

Also, people share similar experiences at times and never know it. You may discover that you are not alone in your circumstances as you develop a God-ordained support network. So, get up! Get going! And be confident!

The "Benjamin" Experience

You have undoubtedly encountered numerous opportunities to sow love or softness in this environment often challenged with negativity. As you 'get going', do not allow opportunities to by-pass you simply because you do not consider yourself "good enough" (presentable / personable, etc.). I further encourage you to not be so involved with your own personal issues that you miss precious opportunities for sharing. You may not be aware of the life circumstances, or life expectancy of the people you come in contact with. These are the people in your world. You have worth and you can make a positive difference in their lives regardless of your current circumstances. Consider the following:

I once knew a man called "Benjamin". Benjamin was a quiet and unassuming man, whom I came in contact with weekly. He led a very private life. Over time, I learned of his struggle with alcoholism and noticed his declining health. At this time, I was preoccupied with my own self-improvement issues. My greetings and communications with him were always kind and polite, but nothing further. One abrupt day, Benjamin was gone. Only his close family and friends knew the actual cause of his passing. In hindsight, I reflected on the missed opportunities to share care and the love of his Creator with Benjamin. I neglected to spend moments expressing concern and encouragement toward Benjamin. Being a task-oriented person, I did not know that Benjamin's tomorrows would not be available to me following the accomplishment of my personal goals.

Do not let my "Benjamin" experience be yours. Encourage the people in your 'world' even while you are focusing on getting 'on track'. Remember that even in the midst of your transition, you have worth and there are people in your world awaiting your smile, appropriate touch, or word of encouragement. You have value and purpose, walk in them. It's your choice.

Press Forward

Without a doubt, there is often someone in our lives who does not want or is not interested in seeing us progress toward the achievement of our Maker's plan and purpose for our lives. Why? The reason for this negative energy is not important. What is important is remembering that we should never count ourselves out when it comes to obtaining the blessings and achievements our Heavenly Father has for us (no matter what our present circumstances are). Sometimes it is necessary to change the way that we do business. If we have taken the road of defeat, it would be necessary to get back on track (i.e. get in position to receive our Creator's best for us).

Additionally, prior compromises of our values or boundaries may have left us physically, emotionally, mentally, or financially vulnerable. We may have experienced damage or loss as a result. Our self-worth may be challenged during what seems to be a loss (or decrease) of control over our circumstances or environment. The walls to our city have been damaged or torn down when we no longer have liberty and/or control; nor do we have the opportunity to be a positive independent influence over our person, life, family, relationships, home, ministry, career, etc. Others now primarily influence our personal boundaries. Certain agencies, programs, officials, or other individuals now establish boundaries and commitments for us. Our ability to govern, protect, and nurture ourselves or significant others in our personal space, is now limited to the significant input of others. Our choices and freedom of movement may be restricted. Trusting our Creator's help in developing a strategy or plan for the essential development and changes needed could be a timely maneuver. Prayer, meditation, reading (God's word – The Bible and books on the subject matter that we are facing): and developing a God-ordained support network could be instrumental in our forward progress. Is it easy to pursue our goals in the face of adversity and opposition? Of course, it is not. Can it be done? Absolutely, is the first response. You decide, is the next response.

The encouraging Biblical passage in Philippians 4:13 reads, "I can do all things through Christ which strengtheneth me".

We also find that God gives the Believers power to be triumphant over all (Luke 10:19). Also, we, as Believers, are more than conquerors (Romans 8:37)

One thing is clear. That is the essential necessity of putting focused *attention* on the desired changes we want in our lives. Once a *strategy* or *plan* has been devised and is ready for implementation, we must be mindful of distractions and hindrances. Also, let's watch out for that feeling of not being quite ready to proceed forward. This uneasiness is perfectly natural particularly if we are treading on new ground (a place of forward progress that we have never been before).

Let's ask ourselves how bad we really want the desired changes. *Qualitative change*may not occur until we are fully convinced that we can no longer tolerate our current situation of fear / defeat. Know that our Creator (God) is not only with us but is able to empower us for forward progress.

The Biblical passage in II Peter 1:3 tells us that God has made available to the Believers "all things that pertain unto life & godliness". We must move forward in faith, not in doubt (Hebrews 10:38). Remember that "God hath not given us the spirit of fear; but of power, and of love, and a sound mind (2Timothy 1:7). You determine the appropriate application.

PART II

Boundaries

Now that you are clear about your desire for forward movement, it is essential that you establish (or re-establish) your boundaries (i.e., evaluate your timing, consider the noise and define your space). Take the time to determine what is important to you. How strong is your desire for forward progress? Consider the lessons you have learned thus far through past / current experiences. Are you really willing to make sacrificial changes (if necessary) in order to reach your desired goals? *No compromising, please.*

Timing

There are several factors involved in the consideration of making changes in our lives to facilitate the fulfillment of our Creator's plan and purpose for us. These factors include, but are not limited to, timing, noise, and space. Time is an essential element of change. The strategy / plan developed for our life's changes will undoubtedly include time frames (immediate, short-term, and long-term goals). These time frames must be realistic if we do not want to set ourselves up for stress-related delay / failure. Time must also be considered in evaluating our current position in achieving our goals. We must remember our individual resources and development in this self-examination. It is imperative that we assess our own individual timing and circumstances, not relying on the comparison of others. Develop a real picture of who you are, where you are, and what you are capable of. (Consider leaving laziness and bashfulness behind if present). If additional knowledge and skills are needed to attain your aspirations, acknowledge this. Yes, of course leave room for divine intervention in your assessment, but do not frustrate yourself further by looking through rose-colored glasses. Again, we are trying to avoid stress-related delay and possible failure.

In both my professional and personal life, I've seen numerous instances of persons embracing unrealistic expectations for themselves and for others. An acceleration of tension, stress, confusion, miscommunication, distress, impatience, and/or physical damage or loss often results from these circumstances. Consequently, maintaining unrealistic expectations may cause you unnecessary delay or loss. Yes, it is okay to dream, but we must be able to delineate the dream from the current reality. We must respond appropriately. Also, in looking at where we are and where we want to go, much patience and diligence may be required. If others are involved, remember to incorporate true loving kindness in your persuasive efforts. Most importantly, allow your Maker, your Heavenly Father, to lead you (into all truth (John 16:13)).

_____

The Biblical passage of Proverbs 3:6 reads, "In all thy ways acknowledge him, and he shall direct thy paths).

_____

Consideration of timing must also be addressed in determining the best time for making your move for change. For example, if there is a plan to obtain housing independence, it may be wise to establish a matching income plan prior to abandoning all ties of housing dependence. (You be the judge of this).

Another consideration would be the timing of our verbalizations during our transitional moments. I am sure that we have all seen the negative consequences of someone burning their bridges, especially prematurely. Remember that your strategy / plan cannot be implemented effectively without patience and wisdom. (Ask your Maker for these if you do not have them). Also, remember that two things hold true in all that you say and do. First of all, today is the first day of the rest of your life. Second, as long as there is breath in your body, you are in the process of becoming. So, encourage yourself to continue pressing forward to your desired goals.

Noise

Noise is another consideration in your forward progress. How many of us live, work, socialize, or conduct business in an environment where there is constant noise (i.e., music, television, conversation, etc.)? Given that we often respond to what we hear, one wonders how much rest or productivity is achieved in these environments. Or, how much time is given to reflection, planning, and evaluating one's position in these environments? How distracted are you? Is it possible to be quiet and 'hear' key thoughts and instructions in the absence of silence and rest? Does your noise level enhance your "aha" experiences (times of heightened enlightenment where answers are realized)? One wonders if these noisy environments are conducive to quality meditation and decision-making. You be the judge.

How have these environments hindered you? How have these noisy environments helped you? I personally maintain that the quieter my environment, the more productive I have become. Certainly, there must be a balance in the sounds we encounter. Look at your current goals, health, and/or circumstances. Weigh the pros and cons of the reduction or increase of noise in your world. Does the noise in your environment enhance your ability to gain / maintain clarity of thought, or does it hinder you by increasing your level of distraction?

Evaluate your 'noise' even further. Do you have control over it? Is it excessive or moderate? What is the purpose of your 'noise'? Are you being entertained, or is the noise simply a cloak? Does the noise provide a haven where necessary thought and communication does not take place; thereby, allowing you to remain inept and unproductive (possibly even deviant)? Consider the energy and emotions elicited by the noise in your environment. Does it afford you the energy and equilibrium you desire?

Noise clearly affects your ability / opportunity to think and rest. Noise also affects your emotions and productivity level. In your plans of getting 'on track' and/or moving forward, consider any practical changes needed with regard to the noise in your environment.

Space

Now, let's define your space:

- First of all, who is in your living space / home?
- Are there children or adults present?
- Do they depend on you in any way?

- Do these individuals require any of your time or space?
- Are you in control of the time you interact with these individuals, or are there mandated duties to perform?
- What space do these individuals occupy in the home?
- How do you feel about this?
- Do you have a place in your home apart from these individuals?
- Do you have appropriate space to plan, evaluate, and work in your home?
- What control do you have over the distractions?
- Are there changes that should or could be made?

Someone once shared that they conduct their business by emotionally and mentally detaching themselves from their partner.

- Are you appropriately connected to the individuals in your living environment (particularly family and friends)?
- What is your focus?
  o If you are a parent and/or spouse, are you still sensitive to the needs and desires of your loved ones?
- Or, have you become hardened or embittered by unresolved situations: and therefore, detached?

I'm sure you've done this before; but take a good look at what has taken place, or what is taking place in your space. Chances are that if dysfunctional relationships have developed, there is a redefinition that needs to take place.

Consider the *roles and communication patterns* of the individuals in your home.

- Are these roles clearly defined and in place?
- What about the communication patterns in the home? Is this communication constructive

and productive, or do you appear to be working at cross-purposes?

- Is one able to rest in your living space?
  - What is the level of peace and respect in this space?
- Are your needs and desires being fulfilled in your home?
- Have the individuals in your 'space' enhanced or hindered your ability to achieve your goals?
- What are the changes or restoration needed? By clearly addressing these issues and related issues, we can begin to bring clarity to our current situation (and, if appropriate, begin providing a foundation for reconstruction).

Another related spatial issue is that of our *belongings.*

- Where are your belongings kept in your home? Do you have the liberty of the entire home, or are there limits to where your belongings are kept? Who determines where your belongings are placed?

- o Are your belongings stationary or moved by others? I am sure that many are aware of key moments lost or delayed due to misplaced or damaged belongings, or from belongings being placed in hard-to-reach places.
- Consider also whether you are responsible for others' belongings in your home (i.e., children, spouse, friends, etc.).
- How much attention is given to the care of these belongings?
- How are your budget and stress level affected by the care of these belongings?
- What adjustments are needed?

Let's also address the level of *privacy* in your living space.

- Is there enough privacy?

- Do you have space for retreat or are you constantly on public display?
    - Is there a clear delineation of where outsiders start and stop?
- If there are others residing in your living space, what are the boundaries?
- What are the rules? Are these appropriate?
    - Are these rules respected?
- What are the consequences for the breach of privacy? Be real for the purposes of clarity.

How much *spatial control* do you have in your living space?
- Do you own your dwelling?
- Who determines what happens in your dwelling and to your dwelling, and how much it costs to live there?
- In evaluating your level of spatial control, consider the previously discussed issues regarding the people in your space, your privacy and belongings.

- o Evaluate the types of challenges that have arisen relating to your spatial control or lack thereof.
- Assess the enhancement or loss in your relationships, resources, health, and mental and emotional well-being resulting from your current level of spatial control.
- What improvement would you benefit from? Could your level of independence be increased? Keep it practical.

Let's discuss your *autonomy* - your sense of self.

- Does your dwelling place depict the "real you"? What level of self-expression is permitted in your dwelling?
- Do you live in an environment that respects your individuality?
- Note your ability to make changes to your environment as desired.

- Consider your level of stability. Are you required to relocate at inopportune times?
- Do you have a place you can actually call home?
- Address your personal values with regard to your environment. Is your environment congruent, or in conflict with your values? (It should be noted that any level of incongruence may cause stress / agitation that would need to be addressed at some point).

In the evaluation of your circumstances, remember that your support network may be able to assist you in problem solving and/or researching other appropriate resources. Be honest and realistic in determining what is important to you. In viewing where you live, whom you want to live with, and owning your home versus sharing this space with others, determine how serious you are about achieving these spatial goals.

Believers, remember your identity in God and his plan and purpose for your life. Determine if your spatial goals agree with God's plan for your life (for true success).

There are encouraging words in the Biblical passage of Jeremiah 29:11 that reads, "For I know the thoughts that I think toward you, saith the Lord, thoughts of peace, and not of evil, to give you an expected end." There is further encouragement in Philippians 4:19 that says, "But my God shall supply all your need according to his riches in glory by Christ Jesus." Numbers 23:19 says, "God is not a man, that he should lie; neither the son of man that he should repent: hath he said, and shall he not do it? Or hath he spoken, and shall he not make it good?" Also remember "…God is able to make all grace abound toward you; that ye, always having all sufficiency in all things, may abound to every good work:"
(2 Corinthians 9:8). Finally, Ephesians 3:20 says that God…" is able to do exceedingly abundantly above all that we ask or think, according to the power that

worketh in us". So, evaluate your circumstances, exercise your faith, and move forward.

There's a familiar scripture that says, "*…faith, without works is dead" (James 2:20).* In other words, you can believe in your abilities, but without exercising and enhancing those abilities, we've accomplished nothing. Now that you have addressed your boundaries of timing, noise, and space let's get to work!

Overcoming Distraction

The manner in which we handle distraction is a key to the accomplishment of our forward progress. Distractions are those *things, words, actions, feelings, conditions, circumstances, etc.* that interrupt or take our attention away from our current focal point. Distractions may come in the form of conflicting thoughts and desires, some misgivings, power struggles, health challenges, crises, rehearsal of bad memories, etc. Take a moment to stop and listen while engaging in self-examination.

Take a look at the way in which you have been handling situations. Would you consider yourself positioned in the reactive mode of putting out fires (addressing things as they reach crisis points), or positioned in the preventative mode (working with a routine that provides more structure and fewer crises)? Now consider your *attitude, reasoning / perceptions, and strategies.* Address any double mindedness (having conflicting opinions), fear, doubt, control issues, self-discipline issues, concerns for loss and grief, etc. Look at the negative ramifications. Are you truly ready for change? Are you ready to move into the space of learning and possibly trying positive things, or is it more comfortable to live with the negative aspects of your past rather than evicting them?

Consider the Biblical verse in Philippians 4:13 that reads, "I can do all things through Christ which strengtheneth me."

The decision must be made because your perspective determines how distractions are handled and at what pace forward progress will take place.

For example, if your goal is to move to a *higher level*, but you are not truly willing to invest the effort necessary for the forward progress, then you may become distracted and embrace the excuses that present themselves. Also, if your goal is to *improve borderline health challenges* through modified eating habits, but you are not engaging in the necessary self-discipline due to various excuses, your goal may not be realized. Finally, if your goal is to *improve the way you relate to loved ones*, but you fear lack of acceptance and respect; the way you respond to excuses as they arise may hinder the achievement of this goal. In other words, distractions occur. The way in which you handle distractions may, in part, determine the length of time it takes, and the amount of energy you have available to achieve your goals. You make the quality decision.

Part III

Can These Bones Live Again?

The consideration of forward progress involves our *view* of our current situation. What is our perception? In instances of financial tension, relationship/familial challenges, health challenges, etc.: the question arises, can these bones live again? Can there be an acceptable resolution and forward progress in my current situation? Is there hope for my situation, or is it too far gone? Consider the biblical depiction of the valley of dry bones (Holy Bible – Ezekiel 37:1-10):

Ezekiel 37:1-10 reads as follows:

[1] The hand of the Lord was upon me, and carried me out in the spirit of the Lord, and set me down in the midst of the valley which was full of bones.

[2] And caused me to pass by them round about: and, behold, there were very many in the open valley; and, lo, they were very dry.

3   And he said unto me, Son of man, can these bones live? And I answered, O Lord God, thou knowest.

4   Again he said unto me, Prophesy upon these bones, and say unto them, O ye dry bones, hear the word of the Lord.

5   Thus saith the Lord God unto these bones; Behold, I will cause breath to enter into you, and ye shall live:

6   And I will lay sinews upon you, and will bring up flesh upon you, and cover you with skin, and put breath in you, and ye shall live; and ye shall know that I am the Lord.

7   So I prophesied as I was commanded: and as I prophesied, there was a noise, and behold a shaking, and the bones came together, bone to his bone.

8   And when I beheld, lo, the sinews and the flesh came up upon them, and the skin covered them above: but there was no breath in them.

9   Then he said unto me, Prophesy unto the wind, prophesy, son of man, and say to the

wind, thus saith the Lord God; Come from the four winds, O breath, and breathe upon these slain, that they may live.

¹⁰ So I prophesied as he commanded me, and the breath came into them, and they lived, and stood up upon their feet, an exceeding great army.

In this passage, the prophet Ezekiel was in a valley full of dry bones. These bones were lifeless. (How would you describe your current situation)? Ezekiel prophesied life to these bones. The bones were indeed restored, but there was a certain process that took place.

1) The bones were first directed to hear the word of the Lord.
   Who are you listening to?

2) The declaration was made.
   What declaration are you making? Is there accountability for your goals?

3) A noise and shaking took place, and the bones moved into their correct places. *What is*

your response to the hint of your restoration (acceptance or digression)?

4) **Sinews, flesh, and skin were produced on these bones.**
   Yes, there are some absolutes necessary for your change.

5) **Breath was given resulting in an army rising and standing on their feet.**
   What will goal achievement mean to you? Consider what happens next (after goal achievement). How bad do you want the change / improvement?

In the valley of dry bones, the restoration of life was complete. Their goal was realized. Keep your goals in view and do not compromise. Keep the meaning of your goals / achievements in view. Further, these bones represented a group of people in the Holy Bible called the Israelites. This was during a time in which they felt dry, hopeless, and segmented due to certain attacks they had suffered. There may be times when you feel so oppressed that your ability

47

to rebuild the walls to your city seems hopeless. With the help and grace of God, restoration and forward movement may take place.

First of all, I believe it is necessary to hear the word of the Lord. Who are you listening to? Who are you identifying with? Yes, you may be limited in stature, resources, level of influence, etc.; but there is a greater one (namely God), who is omnipotent (all-powerful) *(Revelation 19:6),* omniscient (all-knowing) (Psalms 147:3-5; Hebrews 4:12-13), and omnipresent (everywhere present) (Proverbs 15:3; Psalm 139:7-12).

The Biblical passage of Revelation 19:6 reads, "And I heard as it were the voice of a great multitude, and as the voice of many waters, and as the voice of mighty thunderings, saying, Alleluia: for the Lord God omnipotent reigneth."

In the Biblical passage of Psalms 147: 3-5, the writer's reference of God says, "He healeth the broken heart, and bindeth up their wounds." "He telleth the number of the stars, he calleth them all by their names." "Great is our Lord, and of great power: his understanding is infinite."

The Biblical passage of Hebrews 4: 12-13 adds, "For the word of God is quick, and powerful, and sharper than any two-edged sword, piercing even to the dividing asunder of soul and spirit, and of the joints and marrow, and is a discerner of the thoughts and intents of the heart." "Neither is there any creature that is not manifest in his sight: but all things are naked and opened unto the eyes of him with whom we have to do."

Also, Proverbs 15:3 in the Holy Bible reads, "The eyes of the LORD are in every place, beholding the evil and the good."

Finally, the writer of Psalm 139: 7-12 of the Holy Bible provides the following description of God's omnipresence: "Whither shall I go from thy spirit? or whither shall I flee from thy presence?" "If I ascend up into heaven, thou art there: if I make my bed in hell, behold, thou art there." "If I take the wings of the morning, and dwell in the uttermost parts of the sea; even there shall thy hand lead me, and thy right hand shall hold me." "If I say, Surely the darkness shall

cover me; even the night shall be light about me."
"Yea, the darkness hideth not from thee; but the night
shineth as the day: the darkness and the light are both
alike to thee."

Remember Ephesians 3:20 says that God..."is able to
do exceeding abundantly above all that we ask or think,
according to the power that worketh in us." Further,
II Corinthians 9:8 says, "And God is able to make all
grace abound toward you; that ye always having all
sufficiency in all things, may abound to every good
work."

Remember also that you are who your heavenly
father says you are. It's up to you whether you choose
to pursue this identity. Yes, work and sacrifice may
be involved. How bad do you want the change?

Secondly, we must examine what is coming out
of our mouth:

- What are we saying?
- What declarations are we making?

- Are we saying what our Maker says about us, or are we repeating the opinions of others?
- Are we speaking death or life to our situation?
- Are we walking in hope or doubt?

Speak life to your desired goals. As believers, we have the word of God to stand on. There are numerous biblical scriptures that impart the hope of restoration in our lives.

For example, the Biblical story of a man named Job tells of how he suffered in sickness and lost his family members and belongings during a time of testing. Job 42:10 reads, "And the Lord turned the captivity of Job, when he prayed for his friends: also the Lord gave Job twice as much as he had before."

There is a notable protective factor with profitable oversight described in the Biblical passage of John 10:10-12 which reads, "The thief cometh not, but for to steal, and to kill, and to destroy: I am come that they might have life, and that they might have it more abundantly." "I am the good shepherd: the good shepherd giveth his life for the sheep." "But he that is an hireling, and not the shepherd, whose own the sheep are not, seeth the wolf coming, and leaveth the sheep, and fleeth: and the wolf catcheth them and scattereth the sheep."

In another example, the Biblical King named David expressed his restoration walk in Psalms 23, verses 1-3. He first identified his source in verse 1, it reads, "The Lord is my shepherd; I shall not want." King David describes his comfort and provision in verse 2 which reads, "He maketh me to lie down in green pastures: he leadeth me beside the still waters." In verse 3, King David comments on restoration of his inner person, and leadership / direction. Verse 3 reads, "He restoreth my soul: he leadeth me in the paths of righteousness for his name's sake."

A final example addresses fasting and restoration in the Biblical passage of Isaiah 58:11-12 which reads, "And the Lord shall guide thee continually and satisfy thy soul in drought, and make fat thy bones: and thou shalt be like a watered garden, and like a spring of water, whose waters fail not." "And they that shall be of thee shall build the old waste places: thou shalt raise up the foundations of many generations; and thou shall be called, The repairer of the breach, The restorer of paths to dwell in."

~~~~~~~~~~~~~~~~~~~~~~~~~~~~~~~~~~~~~

Now, it is important to determine what foundational belief you base your hope of restoration on. This is a key decision for the subsequent work involved in rebuilding the walls to your city. You determine what *strengthens*, *encourages*, and *empowers* you for forward progress. Be truthful with yourself. Your beliefs will be reflected in your actions.

Thirdly, sound and motion were involved in the restoration of the dry bones. Forward progress was not manifested while the bones were lying still. Sometimes, we may experience an awakening event, or an intensification of circumstances that interrupts our usual response patterns, and helps propel us into the right direction. There may be discomfort due to the unfamiliar ground. What will your next response

53

be? Will it be digression, or acceptance of positive changes?

The fourth transition was the production of sinews, flesh, and skin onto the dry bones. Notice that there was a certain order for the restoration. The bones had to be moved into their correct places for forward progress / growth to take place. We have undoubtedly experienced various transitional events. The question is whether we have moved "out of position" or remained in the right position. We may be able to move forward / grow in our personal development and in attaining our goals when we are "in position" or "in order". Further, the presence of sinews, flesh, and skin on the bones brought the possibility of *multidimensional functioning* (i.e., motion, heating, protection, insulation, strengthening, etc.). The completion of this process was necessary for wholeness. If you are in a barren or 'dry bones' situation, consider the next steps necessary for your forward movement toward a position of *wholeness*. (Your Maker can help you with the insight and sensitivity needed).

For example, if your situation involves a *financial challenge*, consider the immediate steps (not the long-range plans yet) needed to get you back on track. This could include the enlisting of assistance or direction from appropriate businesses / organizations. Effective (not emotional) communication might be an initial step. Quality decision-making regarding budgeting and financial entanglements may also be an immediate consideration.

In a further example where *broken or challenged marital / familial relationships* are present, the initial steps may involve some type of assessment / self-evaluation process. You may begin by considering what you believe to be contributing factors in the challenged relationship and your role in the matter. You may also consider your current desired outcome (i.e., separation, vindication, reconciliation, etc.). Developing short-term goals would be helpful at this time. Consider the ramifications for all parties involved, not just you. Determine what your initial steps would be.

Remember to use your support network and resources in this process.

Finally, consider the initial steps necessary if your *health is challenged*. What will be your functioning level? What is your plan? Remember that commitment, sacrifice, discipline, and consistency are key issues in the plan for restoration. Are you willing to take the appropriate actions?

The final transition involved the restoration of breath / life. These dry bones progressed through the orderly restoration process in a receptive manner. Lengthy processing and hindrances were not presented. The end result was the restoration of an army standing on their feet. The restoration was complete.

As a people, we are free-willed human beings with choices. However, there is an order to the healing, restoration, and/or rebuilding process. Without following the proper order, our life structures may be compromised / weakened. It is not acceptable to receive certain corrections only to refuse the harsh growth experiences in other areas of our lives. Wholeness is our goal. *Challenges may not end at the point of our restoration.* Care is therefore, needed to ensure the reconstruction of a solid foundation in an attempt to avoid the repetition of the current circumstances.

Now it's your turn. Take a good look at yourself, your family, finances, health, etc. Can these bones live again? Is restoration / improvement possible? Consider the following passage:

Death and life are in the power of the tongue: and they that love it shall eat the fruit thereof (Proverbs 18:21).

Evaluate your circumstances. Speak to your situation. Consider your perception and attitude. For the Believers, are you only saying what your Creator says about your circumstances? What scriptures are you standing on?

Proverbs 3:6 reads, "In all thy ways acknowledge him, and he shall direct thy paths."

Now consider even that significant place; the deepest, darkest corner in your life. That place isolated with your most intense moments of frustration, anguish, or emotional discomfort. In this time and place, you are now alone with your Maker in spite of those around you. It's you and your Maker. The One who has seen all and knows all (he's omniscient and omnipresent). Your Maker has been there every step of the way. He is well aware of the choices made. Yes, the One who never sleeps and is all-powerful (omnipotent). What will you do with this time? Cry, release the grief? Please do with wisdom. Do not carry it and allow it to hinder you any further. Request retaliation? It's not profitable. Believers, your Maker already said vengeance was his, he would repay *(Biblical passage of Romans 12:19)*. How will you spend your time?? Walking in bitterness and unforgiveness? This is also unprofitable.

Proverbs 17:22 reads, "A merry heart doeth good like a medicine: but a broken spirit drieth the bones."

What about walking in martyrdom? This is not profitable either. How about remembering who you are; who your Heavenly Father says you are? How about looking at the downed walls of your city and trusting your Maker to help you rebuild and soar (eagle style)?

The Biblical passage of Isaiah 10:31 reads, "But they that wait upon the Lord shall renew their strength; they shall mount up with wings as eagles; they shall run, and not be weary; they shall walk, and not faint."

I am told that the eagle flies higher than the average bird. According to eagleencyclopedia.org, the eagle's wingspan can extend as much as 7 feet or more. Their diet can include live prey. The eagle has very keen vision which allows him to spot his prey high above the intended target. The eagle also puts focused attention on his goal.

- Just like the eagle, purpose in your heart to fly higher (figuratively speaking) than the average response to your situation.
- Rather than walking in discontentment, or learned helplessness, why not govern your thoughts to focus on your future.
- Do not eat the lifeless words of 'limitations', but nourish yourself with the lively 'possibilities' of realistic, positive, growth oriented forward motion.
- Let your positioning / your perspective reflect where you are going and what your goals are. Let your vision, thoughts, and emotions sharpen in discernment and fly high (figuratively speaking) above the current picture, to the revelation of goal achievement. Let's get moving! (If you have already begun forward progress, do not quit).

Let's Go - Push For Excellence

The Declaration of Independence says, "We hold these truths to be self-evident..." (ushistory.org). What is the truth about your life? What is your source? (What do you base your beliefs on)? If you do not base your beliefs on grounded foundational principles, you may set yourself up for failure.

In addressing the Believers' source of hope, the Biblical passage in John 14:6 reads, "Jesus saith unto him [Thomas], I am the way, the truth, and the life: no man cometh unto the Father, but by me." Another Biblical passage addressing belief is found in Hebrew 11:6, which reads, "But without faith it is impossible to please him: for he that cometh to God must believe that he is, and that he is a rewarder of them that diligently seek him."

Consider your belief system.

Julie

I knew a woman named "Julie". Her life and emotions were entangled in a broken/abusive relationship. In speaking with her, she disclosed that her greatest struggle was with the question of whether or not God was real. With further information, Julie became a Believer. She began to study the principles of her Maker. From the point of her acceptance of God as a real being, she began to rebuild the walls of her city. Further, Julie began moving toward the fulfillment of her Maker's plan and purpose for her life. She embraced a belief system upon which she could build her future. You determine in whom you believe. What are you building on? Let's continue.

In your forward progress, consider not only *behavior modification*, but a *qualitative change* in *attitude* and *perception* as well. This is particularly essential if your affairs involve a medical, social, or legal "system" or institution. It is not enough to say, "I am going to do whatever is necessary to resolve this crisis and resume my lifestyle". There may be limitations, but one runs the risk of experiencing a *revolving door* situation in the absence of a qualitative change in attitude and perception. (Marginal change will not suffice). In the revolving door situation, one may encounter similar challenging circumstances over and over again. True resolve and the correct approach are needed.

Look at the *'just enough'* (JE) approach versus the *'positive abundance'* (PA) approach. The JE approach has a limited focus and leaves the door wide open for distractions. The JE approach involves only doing what you are told or exercising minimal effort to achieve one's goals. The minimal level of commitment leaves room for making excuses in response to obstacles, rather than engaging in effective problem-solving behavior. On the other hand, the PA approach may not only focus on exercising the effort necessary for achieving one's goals, but also assisting others simultaneously. The reality is that one's behavior (positive or negative) is affecting others in our world. Why not impact the lives of others positively?

Yes, distractions will manifest and must be dealt with appropriately.

- The emphasis is placed on minimizing distractions; thereby, minimizing the goal-achievement delay.
- Consider prevention focus versus putting out fires.
- Give attention to positive growth and development versus wear and tear on the individual.
- Effective planning and time management activity would be an asset in this area.
- Building up the total man is also an important consideration.

We are not segmented, but whole beings. One with a PA mindset would address the tasks at hand, *and* the following individual *needs*:

- Recreational
- Spiritual
- Nutritional
- Psychological

- Physical, etc.

The essential *focal points* listed below would also be addressed by the individual operating in the PA approach:

- Importance of play
- Spiritual growth
- Psychological growth
- Physical growth
- Personal development
- Eating habits
- Rest habits, etc.

Of course, an imbalance in any of these areas threatens the foundation of our structured lives.

Restoration

Restoration refers to the process of being brought back to a higher level of functioning (or condition) from the current state. The *change* (improvement) may occur in a person, object, place, relationship, situation, etc. The *act* of restoration may be a private individual effort, or an effort supervised by others. Restoration may occur on the level of a single person, or on a group level. Also, the *process* of restoration may yield either positive or negative results. The restoration of family unity would be considered a positive occurrence. On the other hand, the activists' restoration of mayhem may be considered a negative occurrence. For the purposes of this discussion, the term restoration describes the *forward progress of rebuilding one's city walls. Increasing* one's ability to pursue the fulfillment of one's purpose and dreams is the goal intended.

There are Biblical passages that portray restoration (*see below*):

- These passages illustrate the concept of being accepted back by someone following certain changes being made in one's life.
- They also refer to the presence of light being more prevalent than darkness in one's life.
- These passages further portray the transformation from utter abandonment and ruin, to repair and restoration.
- Finally, there is a reference of someone following a people's forward progress until it is completed. (This is what our Maker does for us if we allow him to).

The concept of restoration may seem far-fetched depending on the apparent bleakness or "darkness" in one's circumstances or conditions. One may want to examine whether there is yet time for change.

Isaiah 59:20 reads, "And the Redeemer shall come to Zion, and unto them that turn from transgression in Jacob, saith the Lord."

Isaiah 60:1-2 reads, "Arise, shine; for thy light is come, and the glory of the Lord is risen upon thee." "For, behold the darkness shall cover the earth, and gross darkness the people; but the Lord shall arise upon thee, and his glory shall be seen upon thee."

Further, Isaiah 61:4 reads, "For Zion's sake I will not hold my peace, and for Jerusalem's sake I will not rest, until the righteousness thereof go forth as brightness, and the salvation thereof as a lamp that burneth".

*(Reading the entire passage brings even further inspiration).

A further Biblical reference of restoration is presented as follows:

Jeremiah 29:11-14 reads, "For I know the thoughts that I think toward you, saith the Lord, thoughts of peace, and not of evil, to give you an expected end". "Then shall ye call upon me, and I will hearken unto you. And I will be found in you, saith the Lord: and I will turn away your captivity, and I will gather you from all nations, and from all the places whither I have driven you saith the Lord; and I will bring you again into the place whence I caused you to be carried away captive".

In this passage, there was initial loss. Loss occurs when resources / attributes are violated, or not successfully used for their purposes. Loss may also occur during a time of life darkened by:

- injustices
- violations
- misunderstandings
- exploitations
- frustrations
- hopelessness, etc.

The possibility of restoration and renewal was depicted in this passage. Now you determine what you want your expected end to be. What end will you work toward?

One woman named Betty experienced the reconstruction of the city walls in her life following several:

- hurts

- wrong turns
- disappointments
- losses

She shared that being married and rearing several 'stair step' children (children very close in age), became a challenging yet rewarding process. The reconstruction obviously was not easy. Her family learned to address challenges as *growth opportunities*. They also, as Believers, learned to rely on the instruction and wisdom of their Maker for direction and forward progress. Betty and her family have found that a sound foundation was needed for effective reconstruction.

Remember that the reconstruction process of rebuilding city walls involves much effort and persistence. This process involves:

- work
- determination
- information
- and still more work

The work site must first be cleared to provide space for the redevelopment of a sound foundation. There are issues involving rock and broken concrete that must be removed from the work site and discarded.

- Notice any bitterness and unforgiveness hanging around?
- Is there any anger or hurt cluttering the site?
- What about lack of discipline, obstinacy, apathy, pessimism, etc.; are they hanging around?
- Believers, is there any doubt, fear, or unbelief in God's word or promises lying around?

What caused your walls to fall initially? What can threaten your future walls? What resolutions are needed for forward movement?

Additionally, check the site thoroughly for clutter. It is surprising how clutter seems to:

- cloud vision
- impede clarity of thought
- provide a hiding place for trash and other undesirable elements

Let's address these issues and consider letting go of whatever needs to be discarded. Remember to enlist the assistance of your support system. Also, note that reconstruction can be a wasted effort if true commitments are not adhered to.

Now, let's revisit the effective building materials such as:

- order
- respect
- patience
- self-discipline, etc.

The manner in which these materials, and others, are used may depend on your building technique (laborer, carpenter, and stoneworker) (Lockyer, Sr., H., F. F. Bruce, R. K. Harrison, R. Youngblood, and K. Ecklebarger, 1996. *Nelson's Illustrated Bible Dictionary*. Nashville, T. Nelson).

1) The *laborer* may lay the order, respect, patience, self-discipline, etc. as brick upon brick repetitively.

2) The *carpenter* may use these materials to transform items in their life into usable character, lifestyle, or structure.

3) On the other hand, the *stoneworker* may deal with the harder materials (like procrastination, hatred, unforgiveness, etc.). The stoneworker may isolate the hardened issue with the hammer and wooden pegs of reality and self-truth. Soaking the hardened issues with the liquid of inspiration, love, truth, knowledge, motivation, etc. may result in the stoneworker's production of usable character / building material.

These approaches may be interchangeable depending on the stage of the restoration process. Further, just as there would be with any other building project, there is a Master Builder, our Maker. There are also explicit detailed instructions. Enlist the assistance of your support network for help along this path.

Finally, the 'pity-party' breaks (breaks that indulge in tears, *"why me"*, *"if only"*, *"I would have/could have/should have"*) must be minimized and subsequently loosed. If present, it would be necessary to address:

- selfishness
- disillusionment
- incongruence
- 'grudge-holding'
- unforgiveness

Stay focused! Keep focused attention on what is needed to take care of yourself; of those whom you are responsible for, and on what is needed to accomplish our goals. Remember that you, your family, and your goals are worth fighting for. (You determine if this statement is true).

- o Continue to evaluate your boundaries and timelines.
- o Determine who you are accountable to for checks and balances.
- o Use your support network and resources as needed.

Your Defining Moment; Enough Is Enough

Change is the focus! When does it come? How long do we wait for it? When do we say, "Enough is enough!" During the course of life's journey, we can encounter a myriad of outside influences. These influences range from unfulfilled promises, misdirected advice, inappropriate labeling, and the failure of others to discern your true worth or value. There are also positive influences and precious people who cheer you on as you glide down your pathway to destiny fulfillment and success. The question is what happens when you pause for a moment, assess your surroundings, and realize that somehow your path has changed? You recognize that you have veered away from your goal. What defining moments may assist you in forward motion? Finally, what role does ownership play in the restoration of this journey?

Outside Influences

Janelle notices that her 3 teenage children are no longer energetic and outgoing. They previously buzzed around with endless play, talk of future plans, and boundless questions about life's incongruities and possibilities. What changed? Why is there a posture of silence? What influences navigated a pathway of hopelessness, apathy, learned helplessness, and the like? Janelle now recognizes that her route has somehow changed. She is no longer on the prior path of nurturing her children and their dreams.

The outside influences listed above (i.e. promises (a focal point), advice (input), recognition of your identity (affirmation), and emotional support are some of the factors instrumental in either helping you remain on your chosen path, or distracting you from your chosen path. There may be difficulty encountered in the attempt to control all outside influences. A greater empowerment is our ability to recognize distraction and make informed choices about staying on track with our goals. The Biblical discussion on the story of the alabaster box may bring further enlightenment.

~~~~~~

Luke 7:36-50 reads:

> 36 And one of the Pharisees desired him that he would eat with him. And he went into the Pharisee's house, and sat down to meat.
>
> 37 And, behold, a woman in the city, which was a sinner, when she knew that Jesus sat at meat in the Pharisee's house, brought an alabaster box of ointment,
>
> 38 And stood at his feet behind him weeping, and began to wash his feet with tears, and did wipe them with the hairs of her head, and kissed his feet, and anointed them with the ointment.
>
> 39 Now when the Pharisee which had bidden him saw it, he spake within himself, saying, This man, if he were a prophet, would have known who and what manner of woman this is that toucheth him: for she is a sinner.

⁴⁰ And Jesus answering said unto him, Simon, I have somewhat to say unto thee. And he saith, Master, say on.

⁴¹ There was a certain creditor which had two debtors: the one owed five hundred pence, and the other fifty.

⁴² And when they had nothing to pay, he frankly forgave them both. Tell me therefore, which of them will love him most?

⁴³ Simon answered and said, I suppose that he, to whom he forgave most. And he said unto him, Thou hast rightly judged.

⁴⁴ And he turned to the woman, and said unto Simon, Seest thou this woman? I entered into thine house, thou gavest me no water for my feet: but she hath washed my feet with tears, and wiped them with the hairs of her head.

⁴⁵ Thou gavest me no kiss: but this woman since the time I came in hath not ceased to kiss my feet.

⁴⁶ My head with oil thou didst not anoint: but this woman hath anointed my feet with ointment.

⁴⁷ Wherefore I say unto thee, Her sins, which are many, are forgiven; for she loved much: but to whom little is forgiven, the same loveth little.

⁴⁸ And he said unto her, Thy sins are forgiven.

⁴⁹ And they that sat at meat with him began to say within themselves, Who is this that forgiveth sins also?

⁵⁰ And he said to the woman, Thy faith hath saved thee; go in peace.

Matthew 26:12-13 reads:

¹² For in that she hath poured this ointment on my body, she did it for my burial.

¹³ Verily I say unto you, Wheresoever this gospel shall be preached in the whole world, there shall also this, that this woman hath done, be told for a memorial of her.

The woman in the Biblical account of the alabaster box takes action by approaching Jesus with a valuable substance that she applies to Jesus' feet. This woman symbolically presses beyond her identity (woman with a questionable past). She is not stopped by the possible outside influences of others' opinions of who she is and what she is doing. Her personal convictions define her path, and she moves forward. The woman uses something of worth that is in her possession (the ointment in the alabaster box). The woman applies the ointment to Jesus' feet and wipes his feet with her hair. She uses her hair. (Again, she uses something in her possession that has value). This is her defining moment. She moves from 'the woman with a past' to 'the woman who takes action'. Further, this portion of her story is now made a part of biblical history.

Ownership

In looking at the example of the woman with the alabaster box, we are now encouraged to reflect on our individual situations. What do we have of value within our possession that can assist us in transitioning to the pathway which leads us to goal achievement and destiny fulfillment? What about our attitude? Have outside influences led us to believe that we are 'less than', 'handicapped', 'inhibited', etc.? Has our motivation or inspiration severely decreased? Let's take a moment and make the decision, if necessary, to transition back to our goal achievement and destiny fulfillment pathway. This may be the moment to shift the focus away from negative outside influences back to the affirmation of our identity, our value, and our purpose. Take courage and make each moment count.

Shifting the Seat of Control

(An Exhortation)

Shifting the focus in relationship building may be key for some individuals. Too often we build intimate relationships on the affirmations we receive on some level, only to realize later that we have a serious challenge with the orator. Let's backtrack (i.e., stop, and start again). "What did he (or she) just say"? As a wise Pastor has shared, "Who gave 'him' (or her) the right to define me"? If I am to 'believe what I hear', and actually 'listen' to what this significant other is saying; it may become painfully apparent that - it's time to shift 'the seat of control'.

Too often, we allow people to tell us 'who' we are, and 'where' we are going. (This may not be you; it may be someone you know). While it is true that people encourage us, aid and assist us; why not shift our primary focus to one who has the 'authority' to influence our destiny – our Creator? There's a Biblical passage in Acts 17:28 that reads, "For in him we live, and move, and have our being…" This passage is referring to our Creator. Why are we allowing individuals outside of our relationship with our Creator to have so much influence on determining our destiny? How did they qualify as the authority figure in this area (namely, the area of defining who we are)? Do the individuals with the voices in our ears have our best interests at heart? Are they primarily seeking their own self-gratification at our expense? We have much value and worth given to us by our Creator, who has our best interest at heart. Is this significant individual in this relationship encouraging us to grow and develop in a manner that enables us to leave a valuable legacy for others? Is our focus in this relationship defense / compromise, or growth and fulfillment? It may be time for a shift in focus.

No, this is not a 'girls you do not need men' (or 'child, you do not need anyone') message. This is a let's focus on our motives, get healed of our hurts, truly listen when that special someone discloses a history of harshness, addictions, or other dysfunctional history; and let's begin new relationships with a healthier start.

"Who am I"? "What do I want to do"? "Who do I want to be when I grow up"? As little girls (and boys), we begin addressing these questions in our childhood. Some have clearer answers than others. Different facets of these questions permeate our youth and remain with us in adulthood.

We may begin gaging our success in stability by the self-realization, definition, affirmation, and awards received along this life's journey. But wait! What happens when this process is interrupted by a voice louder than our own? What happens when a significant individual establishes themselves in a close relationship with us, and then begins feeding us actions and words of negativity – yes, even harshness and misuse? What happens when this relationship becomes an entangled maze with much darkness and very little light? How does one literally dig themselves out of the cave of misperceptions?

First, it would be important to initiate a plan of safety that includes the element of accountability.

Allowing 'helping professionals' to give input into the situation would be appropriate since we were not created as an island – we need each other. When the dust has settled and personal care has taken place, we can begin to assess our motives and boundaries in relationships. "Who am I"? "What do I want to do"? Who do I want to be"? "Am I that person"? Yes, these questions still need to be answered. Let helping professionals provide assistance. And this time, why not let our Creator's voice be the loudest voice – shift the 'seat of control'? For it is through our Creator that we would be guided 'into all truth' – even self-truth (as found in the Holy Bible).

Fighting For Existence

Making Room For "Me"

Consider the following:

An expectant mother spends the next several weeks dealing with transition after the conception of a child. Morning sickness, emotional upheaval, and other uncharacteristic occurrences signal the invasion of a foreign body in the mother's internal structure. There is seemingly an initial fight to determine if the mother's body will accept or reject this new development. As the pregnancy progresses, adjustments are made to provide further room for the unborn child's growth and development. Additionally, the umbilical cord works steadily to nurture this new being. Finally, the time for delivery arrives and the umbilical cord is no longer needed.

Fighting for existence does not only take place in the mother's womb. Our birthing process in and of itself is an awesome wonder. From the time we take our first breath, we encounter numerous hurdles. Challenges thread our existence as we pursue the right to be ourselves. We either move forward with strength, or experience delay through weakness. Hindrances may have occurred along the way to circumvent our pursuit of vision and dream fulfillment. As we press beyond our past toward our future, let's rebuild the walls to our cities. Let's transition from a place of defeat to a place of forward progress. *Stay in the fight! Let's win!*

Exhortation

We know that we are living in trying times. Believers, know that we have dependable help because we can trust our Maker in everything concerning us.

Psalm 91:1-2 reads, "He that dwelleth in the secret place of the most high shall abide under the shadow of the almighty". "I will say of the Lord, he is my refuge and my fortress: my God: in him will I trust".

There's a special place that we can go in God. No matter what the situation may be, there is none that can take away the trust we have in God.

It should be noted that when we speak of rebuilding the walls to our cities, we may first want to consider our originator. We may first want to acknowledge our Maker as the chief builder and protector.

Psalm 127:1 puts it best, it states, "Except the Lord build the house, they labor in vain that build it: except the Lord keep the city, the watchman waketh but in vain".

(You determine if this is true for you).
According to this, our cities can effectively be kept by our great and mighty God who never sleeps nor slumbers; the God who is omnipotent, omnipresent, and omniscient.

In Isaiah 43:2, God said that he would be with us when we pass through the waters, the rivers would not overflow us, and we would not be burned. The flame would not kindle upon us when we walked through the fire".

Again, the situations we encounter from day to day may be very challenging at times, but we know that we can continue to move forward if we keep our faith and trust in our Maker.

Isaiah 26:2-4 reads, "Open ye the gates that the righteous nation which keepeth the truth may enter in".

"Thou wilt keep him in perfect peace, whose mind is stayed on thee". "Trust thee in the Lord forever: for the Lord Jehovah is everlasting strength".

You are encouraged to determine what your source of faith and encouragement is. Assess the firmness of your foundational beliefs as forward motion toward restoration continues.

Transition

Joshua 5

A biblical passage in the 5th chapter of the book of Joshua talks about the activity of a group of people called the Children of Israel. They had transitioned into a new territory which was later called Gilgal. This group was transitioning from their past oppression and moving toward their future hope.

The men underwent circumcision during this transition. There was a process of 'letting go' of the old ways, as an allegiance and unification began to take place. A time of healing and strengthening took place, as the group paused in their journey. These actions facilitated growth in this group being able to eat from the land of their new territory.

- What actions facilitate growth during your transitions?
- Does your change involve the process of 'letting go' of behaviors, or some things?
- What boundaries are necessary?

- Is there a desired time of healing and strengthening?
- Is there an essential unification or congruence?

Some situations involve a reckoning of the past, and the dawning of a new beginning. Stay focused!

Day of Reckoning - Day of New Beginning

Cynthia's gaze fixed on the side profile of her husband John's face as the Judge rendered their *foreclosure* judgment. Cynthia could look at no one else due to her racing emotions and thoughts. Cynthia and John knew that this was their day of reckoning; as well as, their day for new beginnings.

Cynthia and John had moved into their home when Cynthia was four months pregnant. John had promised Cynthia that their first child would not be born in an apartment. (Cynthia initially had noise and spatial concerns).

John and Cynthia both had good jobs. Their ongoing strife and contention overshadowed the joy of living in their new home. Many warnings were spoken. John and Cynthia heeded none of them. Cynthia continued her campaign of arguments, disobedience toward sound instruction, and unforgiveness, while John continued doing as he pleased.

Through a series of bad choices, John and Cynthia found themselves without stable walls. The walls to their city involved their homeownership, marriage, employment, church affiliation, family, and friends. Their homeownership helped John and Cynthia establish convenient public and private boundaries. They no longer had this luxury as renters. The upheaval challenged the direction of John and Cynthia's marriage. John and Cynthia obviously could not continue their way of doing business if they wanted any measure of success.

They made a decision to repent for their wrongdoings and to move forward in unity. Additionally, a wise prophetic woman of God in their church admonished them not to look back. They were directed to hold no regrets as they moved forward. Heeding these wise instructions immediately closed the door to the blame game and saved John and Cynthia precious time in the rebuilding process. John and Cynthia again became homeowners in less than ten years. They also greatly matured in their marriage and as believers (a continuous process).

Again, rebuilding the walls to one's city involves *focused attention*. The success described above was due in part to the focused attention. Another important process involved in restoration is *addressing the issues*. The healing of emotions and the hunt for disruptive / unresolved situations also needs to take place. Let's take a look at this process.

Healing to Build

Have you noticed that during the process of rebuilding the walls to your city, there appears to be a delay in the restoration process? There may be other factors present; however, this is a good time to rule out the possibility of the presence of strong emotions which appear to be lying dormant. The emotions in question may be:

- anger
- frustration
- the rehearsal of loss
- unresolved unforgiveness, etc.

I will share the following example to demonstrate the strength of these emotions:

I was told of a young lady who had experienced a distressing situation which resulted in the above emotions. She was affected to the point that she would walk around jerking and stating to an unknown entity, "Get off of me." She described the experience of feeling as though 'something' was biting her.

Are any of the above emotions 'eating' at you, or someone you know? These emotions can not only adversely affect your health, but they can also significantly reduce the pace of your forward progress toward goal fulfillment. If your goal is to fulfill your purpose/destiny ordained by your Creator, you may find that it is time to 'let go' of the above emotions. Let's work on accomplishing this.

- Don't forget to enlist the assistance of your God-ordained support network. (i.e., counselors, parents, mentors, etc.).
- Also, remember to make yourself accountable to someone in your support network while moving forward toward goal achievement.
- Finally, keep making progress in your rebuilding efforts since healing and restoration are processes.

Making the choice to move forward is yours. This process may even involve a bit of hunting as described below. *Let's win!*

It's Hunting Season

It may be necessary to hunt, to seek out those emotions or unresolved situations in your life which are now holding you back. These emotions or situations may have caused you loss (loss of time, resources, relationships, freedom, etc.). Let's take the time to hunt for the root causes and deal with the sources of this disruption. Are we looking at:

- fear
- lack of information
- lack of discipline
- doubt
- low self-esteem, etc.

When the roots are dealt with, we can move forward to recovery and restoration. (Allow your God-ordained support network to assist you with this).

There's a Biblical scenario found in chapters 29 & 30 of I Samuel which talked about how a king named David and his men suffered the attack / burning of their dwelling place, called Ziklag. King David and his men also suffered the loss of their wives and children, who were taken captive, while King David and his men were away preparing to fight a battle along with the Philistines. These attackers, a group called the Amalekites, had chosen to invade King David's territory in his absence. *(Notice any personal areas you have left unattended due to unresolved issues (i.e. finances, relationships, goals, etc.))? (Let's take the time to focus on those personal areas).*

King David and his men were sent home by the Philistines prior to their battle. The Philistines did not want King David's help because they were concerned that King David would turn on them due to unresolved issues from a prior battle. When King David and his men returned home to Ziklag and saw what had taken place, they were highly distraught. There was much weeping and talk of stoning King David. King David then enlisted the help of his support network and inquired of his God what his next action should be regarding restoration.

I Samuel 30:8 reads, "And David inquired at the Lord, saying, Shall I pursue after this troop? Shall I overtake them? And he answered him, Pursue: for thou shalt surely overtake them, and without fail recover all."

King David followed the advice and was victorious in his goal achievement. Their families and goods were restored. This ending may not have happened if King David did not have the courage to seek appropriate instruction and resolve in a horrendous situation. He could have chosen various options which may have involved an easier path. He actually won after seeking the path which produced forward motion. Rooting out disruptive emotions or unresolved situations, (with the aid of your support network), requires focused attention.

Are you willing to hunt? Are you wearing protective gear for adversarial circumstances? What plan is being developed to achieve forward motion toward restoration?

Wearing Protective Gear

The biblical passage of Ephesians 6:10-18 addresses the consideration of wearing protective gear while dealing with adversarial situations.

Ephesians 6:10-18 reads:

10 Finally, my brethren, be strong in the Lord, and in the power of his might.

11 Put on the whole armour of God, that ye may be able to stand against the wiles of the devil.

12 For we wrestle not against flesh and blood, but against principalities, against powers, against the rulers of the darkness of this world, against spiritual wickedness in high places.

13 Wherefore take unto you the whole armour of God, that ye may be able to withstand in the evil day, and having done all, to stand.

14 Stand therefore, having your loins girt about with truth, and having on the breastplate of righteousness;

¹⁵ And your feet shod with the preparation of the gospel of peace;

¹⁶ Above all, taking the shield of faith, wherewith ye shall be able to quench all the fiery darts of the wicked.

¹⁷ And take the helmet of salvation, and the sword of the Spirit, which is the word of God:

¹⁸ Praying always with all prayer and supplication in the Spirit, and watching thereunto with all perseverance and supplication for all saints;

The need to address strength, power, and armor / protective gear are highlighted. Without going into a full discussion, it is clear that it is important to clearly identify the adversary - the wind behind the wave, if you will. What is the root cause of the negative situation? Is there a change in posture involved? What's happening with that? What are the ramifications?

The areas identified for protective covering were the loins, upper torso, feet, head area, and all other areas blocked by a shield. The components of the protective gear included, but were not limited to truth, breastplate of righteousness, the 'preparation of the gospel of peace', shield of faith, helmet of salvation, and sword of the Spirit (aka the Bible - word of God). This passage also included the exercise of prayer. While this was described from a biblical perspective, it does highlight the need to consider protective covering. What is it that you rely on as a stabilizing factor in adversarial circumstances? What empowers you? What are your values, constraints, and boundaries? What do you have control over (ex. put on, put off /get rid of)? What enables you to operate both in offense and in defense when necessary?

Finally, let's take a look at our focus and our fruit in adversarial territory (i.e., on the hunt). The biblical passage of Psalms 23:5a reads:

Thou preparest a table before me in the presence of my enemies....

Let's look at that concept - preparing a table before you in the presence of your enemies.

What would that table look like? What would the table look like if the fruit of the Spirit were present? The biblical passage of Galatians 5:22-23 references attributes like:

- Love
- Joy
- Peace
- Longsuffering
- Gentleness
- Goodness
- Faith
- Meekness
- Temperance

If one ate from these fruits and the seeds multiplied from these fruits in the presence of our enemies: I wonder how the enemies like depression, anger, strife, contention, lack, poverty, control, manipulation, delay, hindrances, confusion, and the like would be addressed? ...a table prepared for us, by our Shepherd, in the presence of our enemies.... I wonder if our confidence and focus would be more on what our Shepherd was doing, rather than on what the enemies were doing? I wonder if the fruit on that table would be designed to sustain us against the assignments of our enemies? Finally, I wonder if the nourishment on that table would be geared to facilitate the fulfillment of our destiny / purpose? What do you think? Where is your focus, on the potential fruit influenced by your Creator or on the restrictions of your challenge?

Part IV

Completion: The Song

In this story, the singer is going forth in song and comes to the next stanza. This stanza is key for the song and somewhat challenging. The vocalist does not want to make an error in singing the next key. There is a significant pause noted by the audience. All are watching. The musician is baffled and wonders what the singer will do next. The musician fills in this space with complementary cords, to save the moment. Then, the vocalist opens her mouth trusting that the pitch will be accurate as she proceeds with the next stanza. All is well. The melody is pleasant. The audience resumes their spirited participation.

The singer has experienced her accomplishment of introducing and completing the challenging song. The vocalist could have stopped in the middle of the song and apologized for her ineptitude, but she pursued her goal and achieved it. By the same token, your goals and challenges may involve risks. Now it's your turn to decide if you will

choose to accept the challenges. Will you seriously
work on overcoming the obstacles to make success
possible?

Prove Him Now

(An Exhortation)

We would love to live in a world where there are no serious challenges. However, the reality is that there are some circumstances that may occur which threaten to not only shake, but also totally destroy your very foundation (i.e., your ability to live and breathe, or your reason for living). Circumstances may arise which challenge your established core values, threaten to shift sound paradigms, attack your well-being or the provision of your basic necessities of life (i.e., food, clothing, and shelter); or even hinder your very expression of trust, love and affection. I have experienced such a similar situation. I did not know exactly what the outcome would be, but I knew that, "I WON" and so did my family. As I lay down at night and I awakened in the morning, I did not know what each moment would bring. This was my walk of faith. I did know; however, that I could lie down in peace because my Maker was my refuge as referenced in the Biblical passage of Psalms 91:1-2.

Psalms 91:1-2 reads, "He that dwelleth in the secret place of the most High shall abide under the shadow of the Almighty." "I will say of the LORD, He is my refuge and my fortress: my God; in him will I trust."

When I arose in the morning, I could truly say that this was the day that the Lord had made; I am rejoicing and I am glad in it. (As expressed in the Biblical passage of Psalm 118:24). Because my Maker was the center of my life, I found encouragement in Psalm 93:4,5, which read:

"The Lord on high is mightier than the noise of many waters, yea, than the mighty waves of the sea". "Thy testimonies are very sure: holiness becometh thine house, O Lord, forever".

Further, the promises in Psalm 92:13-15 read:

"Those that be planted in the house of the Lord shall flourish in the courts of our God".

"They shall still bring forth fruit in old age: they shall be fat and flourishing;
To shew that the Lord is upright: he is my rock, and there is no unrighteousness in him".

Let's also visit Isaiah 43:1-3a:

"But now thus saith the Lord that created thee, O Jacob, and he that formed thee, O Israel, fear not: for I have redeemed thee, I have called thee by thy name; thou art mine".
"When thou passest through the waters, I will be with thee; and through the rivers, they shall not overflow thee: when thou walkest through the fire, thou shalt not be burned; neither shall the flame kindle upon thee".
"For I am the Lord thy God, the Holy One of Israel, thy Saviour..."

You may want to address the question of whom you have identified as being your redeemer. How solid is your foundation? I know my purpose. I yet have work to do. Each day brings another opportunity to see my Maker's best fulfilled in my life. I would love to find that your Maker's best is being fulfilled in your life as well. Go forth! Let's win!

The Eye of The Storm

Amid that harsh, tumultuous, or bleak picture, one can search for that place of peace. Consider the following discussion on the eye of the storm:

Serious challenges or upheavals may be referred to as storms. Life's storms experienced by many may be characterized by the occurrences associated with natural impactful events like hurricanes or tropical cyclones. Hurricanes / tropical cyclones are devastatingly violent storms with intense winds, flooding, and rains (nationalgeographic.org). Property loss or the loss of life may result from these very costly, unsettling, and dangerous events. Right in the midst of the massive torrential rains and powerful fierce winds, an incredible occurrence takes place. This event is known as the formation of the *eye of the storm* (britannica.org).

A special reflection is found in 2 Corinthians 3:17b which reads, "...where the Spirit of the Lord is, there is liberty."

In looking at the peace in the eye of the storm, one realizes that it is possible for a calm to exist in the midst of major turmoil. During experiences such as financial crisis, major health challenges, family dysfunction, work-place upheaval, malcontent, etc., it is reassuring to note that there can be a stabilizing force: a place of centering, even in the presence of life's negative factors. There's a phenomenal centering of energy in the eye of the storm. What's happening in the center of your life? In the midst of the obvious commotion, disruption, or other intensified activity; is there a place of rest, a peaceful meditation? Where is your focus? Yes, it may take additional effort, but the reward of reaching that place of calm / peace is immeasurable.

Some may find that calm / peace by closely associating with the multiple facets / names of their Creator, their Maker. The 12 Steps of Alcoholics Anonymous refers to the Higher Power as we understand Him. (Bill W. (1955). "Alcoholics Anonymous: the story of how many thousands of men

and women have recovered from alcoholism"
(2nd ed.). New York City: Alcoholics Anonymous
World Services).

I would like to point out that he may be understood
as:

- Our provider, healer, shepherd
- Almighty God, The Most High God
- The God who sees, our peace, our banner
- Omnipotent God, Omniscient God, Omnipresent God
- The Lord of Hosts
- The God that is more than enough
- And so much more (Holy Bible, King James Version (KJV), Public Domain).

This is not a panacea for all ills. Core values, conduct,
relationship, culture, and behavior, etc. are discussed
in a historical book of instruction, the Holy Bible.

There is reassurance in the biblical passage of Psalm
91 which reads:

1 *He that dwelleth in the secret place of the most High shall abide under the shadow of the Almighty.*

2 *I will say of the LORD, He is my refuge and my fortress: my God; in him will I trust.*

3 *Surely he shall deliver thee from the snare of the fowler, and from the noisome pestilence.*

4 *He shall cover thee with his feathers, and under his wings shalt thou trust: his truth shall be thy shield and buckler.*

5 *Thou shalt not be afraid for the terror by night; nor for the arrow that flieth by day;*

6 *Nor for the pestilence that walketh in darkness; nor for the destruction that wasteth at noonday.*

7 *A thousand shall fall at thy side, and ten thousand at thy right hand; but it shall not come nigh thee.*

8 *Only with thine eyes shalt thou behold and see the reward of the wicked.*

9 *Because thou hast made the LORD, which is my refuge, even the most High, thy habitation;*

10 *There shall no evil befall thee, neither shall any plague come nigh thy dwelling.*

11 *For he shall give his angels charge over thee, to keep thee in all thy ways.*

12 *They shall bear thee up in their hands, lest thou dash thy foot against a stone.*

13 *Thou shalt tread upon the lion and adder: the young lion and the dragon shalt thou trample under feet.*

14 *Because he hath set his love upon me, therefore will I deliver him: I will set him on high, because he hath known my name.*

15 *He shall call upon me, and I will answer him: I will be with him in trouble; I will deliver him, and honour him.*

16 *With long life will I satisfy him, and shew him my salvation.*

―――――――――――――――――――――――

Finally, how many times has the statement been made, "If only I could get beyond this point in my life, I could move forward"? "If only..." "If only..." Why not press beyond the *reactive mode* of waiting for the "If onlys" to take place and begin the *proactive motion* of making quality decisions, or taking purposeful action even while you are attending to your urgent matters? In spite of the distractions and delays, plan and wisely seek opportunities to move forward to your next level of goal achievement. Meanwhile, if you are currently facing intense circumstances / turmoil that challenge your forward progress, may you discover that place of peace / calm in the eye of the storm.

Endnote (Choices)

In this season, we get to:

1) **CHOOSE** - We get to determine what we want. No one can take our desire from us. We decide what we attribute 'worth' or 'value' to.

2) **DECIDE** what it takes to get what we want. We get to assess the cost of our desire, establish the necessary actions, and evaluate its worthiness.

3) **TAKE THE ACTION** either to fully pursue what it is that we want, or where wisdom prevails; make an actionable plan that is congruent with our desire seasoned with wisdom. Then we may take measured, consistent steps toward goal achievement and review.

Does this sound familiar even in the new season?
Let's focus and Let's win!

Endnote - Invitation

Throughout this book, I have referenced a group known as Believers. These are individuals who have acknowledged the Fatherhood and Headship of God, their Creator and Maker in their lives. These individuals have also acknowledged His Son Jesus as Lord and Savior of their lives. They have received promises including the gift of eternal life. Here are biblical passages that expound on this:

Romans 3:23 reads: "For all have sinned, and come short of the glory of God."
Romans 6:23 adds: "For the wages of sin is death; but the gift of God is eternal life through Jesus Christ our Lord."
John 3:16-17 reads: "For God so loved the world, that He gave his only begotten Son, that whosoever believeth in him should not perish, but have everlasting life. For God sent not his Son into the world to condemn the world; but that the world through him might be saved."

Ephesians 2:8-9 explains: "For by grace are ye saved through faith; and that not of yourselves it is the gift of God." "Not of works, lest any man should boast."
I Peter 2:24 reads: "Who his own self bare our sins in his own body on the tree, that we, being dead to sins, should live unto righteousness: by whose stripes ye were healed."
Romans 10:9-10 reads: "That if thou shalt confess with thy mouth the Lord Jesus, and shalt believe in thine heart that God hath raised him from the dead, thou shalt be saved." "For with the heart man believeth unto righteousness; and with the mouth confession is made unto salvation."

You are invited to pray the following prayer if you too want to become a Believer:
LORD Jesus, please forgive me for all of my sin. I believe with my heart that you, Jesus died on the cross and that God raised you from the dead. I ask you to be my Savior and Lord. I am now saved.

You are then encouraged to attend / connect with a Bible believing church for further instruction, support, and fellowship / association.

The Next Chapter Begins with You

(Journal Invitation)

Notes

▪Goals: (i.e., Re-establishing personal boundaries, financial reset, health reset, social reset, pending achievements, etc.)

▪Action Items / Deliverables / Timelines:

(New business, unfinished business, breaking things down into bite-sized pieces, accountability through timelines)

▪Assessment / Evaluation:

▪Repeat/ Clarification/ Moving Forward:

▪Legacy Production:

(Beginning with your end-goal. Who do you want to impact? How do you want to be remembered ...)?

The Next Chapter Begins with You

(Journal Invitation)

Notes (continued)

The Next Chapter Begins with You

(Journal Invitation)

Notes (continued)

ABOUT THE AUTHOR

C.S. Bayliss (pen name), M. A. Community/Clinical Psychology has served the public in the field of Social Work for over 25 years. She has been married for over 29 years and is the mother of 5 biological adult children, 1 wonderful adult bonus daughter, and grandchildren. C. S. Bayliss has also served as ministry support in her church for over 20 years. She continues to operate in her roles as mother, daughter, wife, grandmother, professional, and helper.